Have a question or concern? Let us know.
FritzenPublishing.com | support@fritzenpublishing.com

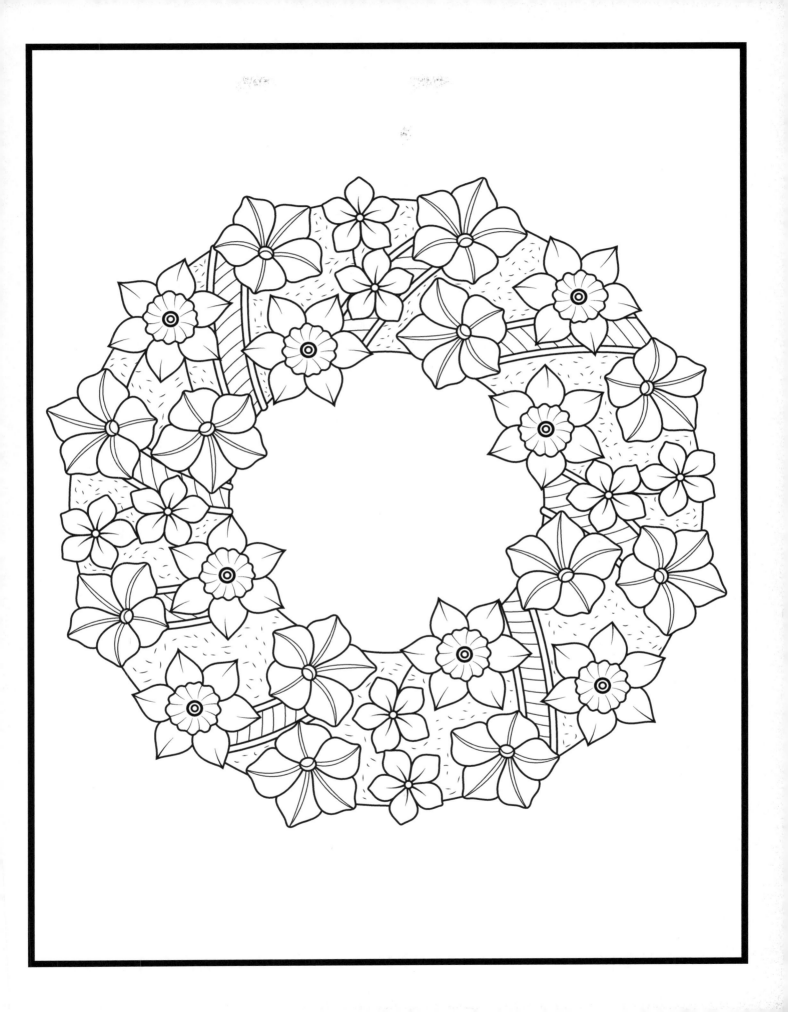

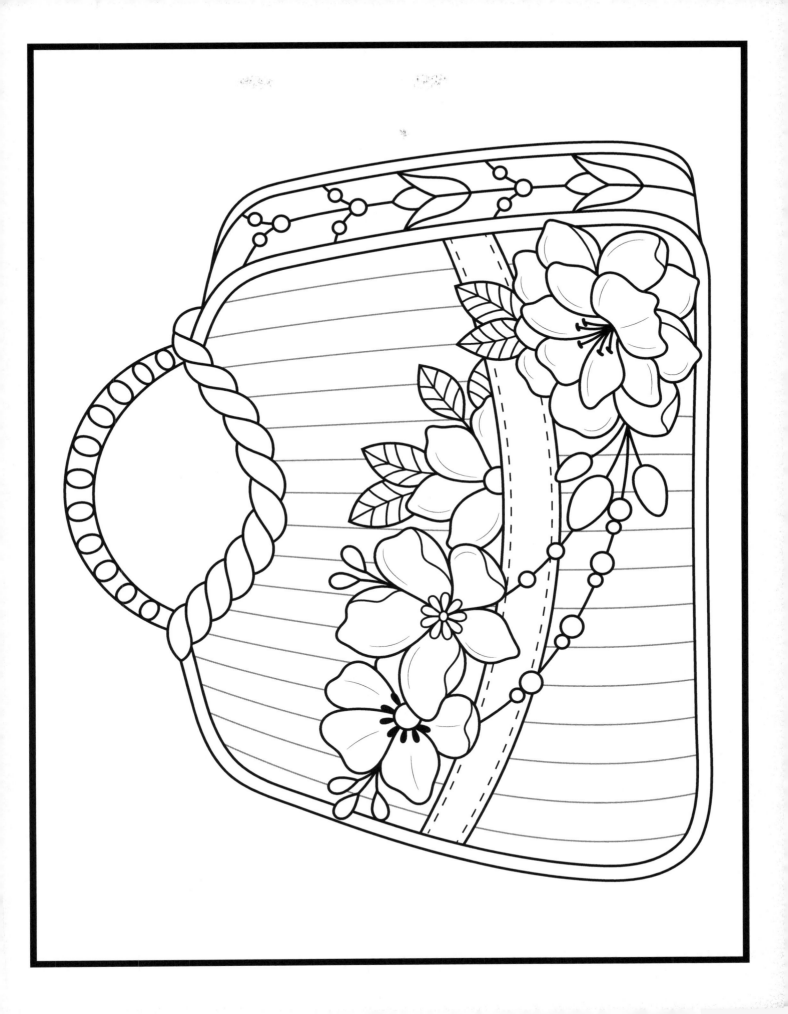

BUY DIGITAL EDITIONS

Shop now on JadeSummer.com.

Download PDF versions. Use your favorite paper.
Color unlimited times. Never wait for shipping.

JOIN OUR EMAIL LIST

Join now on JadeSummer.com.

Be the first to know about new releases.
Don't miss out on sales and important updates.

JOIN OUR ARTWORK GROUP

Search for *Jade Summer Artwork* on Facebook.

View and share completed pages.
Participate in online events. Make new friends.

100 Animals	Christmas Animals	Easter
100 Flowers	Christmas Flowers	Emoji
Adorable Owls	Christmas for Kids	Fairies
Alice in Wonderland	Christmas for Toddlers	Fantasy Adventure
Amazing Patterns	Christmas Mandalas	Fantasy Collection #1
Ancient Egypt	Christmas Patterns	Fantasy Collection #2
Animal Mandalas (2018)	Color Charts	Fantasy Grayscale
Animals for Beginners	Costume Cats	Fantasy Kids
Anime	Country Cabins	Flower Bouquets
Art Nouveau	Country Cats	Flower Girls
Autumn	Country Farm	Flower Mandalas
Baby Dragons	Country Romance	Flowers for Beginners
Beach Homes	Cute Animals	Forest Animals
Beautiful Birds	Cute Animals #2	Graffiti Animals
Beautiful Flowers	Cute Cats	Greatest Hits (2019)
Beginner Collection	Cute Christmas	Greek Mythology
Chibi Animals	Cute Fairies	Grimm Fairy Tales
Chibi Girls #1	Cute Fairies Grayscale	Haunted House
Chibi Girls #2	Cute Unicorns	Hidden Garden
Chibi Girls Grayscale	Cute Witches	Halloween
Chibi Girls Horror	Dark Fantasy	Horses
Christmas #1	Delicious Food	Inspirational Collection
Christmas #2	Dragons	Inspirational Quotes
Christmas #3	Dreams Come True	Inspirational Words

LEAVE YOUR AMAZON REVIEWS

Show your support for Jade Summer and help other colorists discover our artwork.

Simply find this book on Amazon, scroll to the reviews section, and click "Write a customer review".

Thank you for your purchases and reviews.

Made in the USA
Middletown, DE
04 April 2020